Patrick Donan, Chicago Burlington & Quincy Railroad
Company

The Heart of the Continent

An Historical and descriptive treatise for business men, home seekers, and

tourists, of the advatages, resources, and scenery of the great West

Patrick Donan, Chicago Burlington & Quincy Railroad Company

The Heart of the Continent

An Historical and descriptive treatise for business men, home seekers, and tourists, of the advatages, resources, and scenery of the great West

ISBN/EAN: 9783337194703

Printed in Europe, USA, Canada, Australia, Japan

Cover: Foto ©Andreas Hilbeck / pixelio.de

More available books at **www.hansebooks.com**

THE HEART

OF THE

CONTINENT

THE HEART OF THE CONTINENT:

*AN HISTORICAL AND DESCRIPTIVE TREATISE
FOR BUSINESS MEN, HOME SEEKERS AND
TOURISTS, OF THE ADVANTAGES,
RESOURCES AND SCENERY*

OF THE

GREAT WEST.

PUBLISHED BY THE PASSENGER DEPARTMENT
CHICAGO, BURLINGTON & QUINCY RAILROAD.

CHICAGO, ILL.
1882.

THE HEART OF THE CONTINENT.

I.

The Immensity and Grandeur of the American Great West.

"I never felt as if I was out of doors before," exclaimed a New England man, as he stepped off the cars, for the first time, west of the Mississippi; and it was a natural expression of amazement and admiration at the new sensations of vastness and grandeur that had come over him. To one from the petty kingdoms and duchies of the Old World, many of them scarcely larger than a Nebraska or Colorado county, it is impossible to convey any idea of the boundless immensity of our American Great West.

To one from the small and over-crowded regions of the New England and other Eastern States, a trip through the vast, vigorous, growing empire of the West and Southwest is full of interest and instruction. It is a whirling panorama of perpetual contrasts and surprises — a lightning express train of magnificent scenes and ever-novel facts and ideas. He finds that all he has heretofore heard or read has failed to convey even a faint conception of its extent and resources, and that in order to properly comprehend its greatness he must begin anew and learn from observation. He has regarded the northern shores of Ohio and Illinois, or the remoter confines of Iowa and Nebraska as the *Ultima Thules* of the American Republic. What is his amazement to discover that his diminutive province is but a speck on the mighty map of America, and that north and west of Illinois,

Iowa and Nebraska stretches thousands of miles away a realm equally as vast as all that lies east and south of them to the Atlantic and the Gulf of Mexico.

After voyaging up the majestic Mississippi, nearly fifteen hundred miles from the delta where Eads has planted his jetties,

View of Michigan Avenue, Chicago.

he reaches Keokuk or Burlington in what, scarce a generation ago, was an unknown land, and thinks now he has certainly reached the utmost verge of civilization. But he soon learns that he has only entered the gateway to the great imperial western domain that still rolls away in an unending glorious vista of prairie and woodland, mountain, lake and magnificent river, city, village, mines, field and meadow, that reach to the golden shores of the Pacific.

He rambles on for hundreds of miles, north or west or south, and at every halting-point thinks he is at the jumping-off place of creation. It takes four figures to measure the miles that lie between him and any spot he has ever known before, and he is convinced that there cannot be any more country beyond. But, at every turn, on every hand, he hears of illimitable regions yet ahead of him; of the marvelous fertility of the valleys of the Platte, the Republican, the Rio Grande and the Colorado; of horizon-fenced plains of grass and grain in Kansas, Nebraska and Wyoming, where a nation with all its flocks and herds may find sustenance; of mines yet to be opened up in Colorado, Montana, Idaho, Arizona, New Mexico and California, that shall surpass all the boasts of Ophir and of Ind, and make the colossal fortunes of all the Goulds and Vanderbilts of to-day seem trivial by comparison; of rich pastures and wheat lands stretching away on the south-west to the confines of "the land of the Montezumas;" of regions scarcely yet unexplored, but known to be as beautiful and productive, and as capable of supporting millions of industrious population, as the fairest gardens of Illinois, Iowa and Nebraska.

At Omaha, the Shadowland of legend and romance of less than forty years ago, he hears of steamboats running regularly two thousand miles further up the Missouri and six hundred up the Yellowstone; of navigating the Saskatchewan, Winnipeg and the Lake of the Woods, and other streams whose names he never heard before, flowing thousands of miles into Hudson's Bay, Puget Sound and the Arctic Ocean. He hears of harbors like those of Portland, Vancouver, San Francisco, San Diego and Guaymas, in which all the commerce of the world may safely ride at anchor.

He sees long lines of railway whose iron tracks span the untrod wilderness of half a generation ago. He sees single wheatfields, amid what were laid down in the geographies of but a decade ago as alkali deserts, broader than Old-World principalities, waving with golden harvests whose luxuriance has amazed all Christendom. He hears the thunder of the greatest gold and silver mills in the world resounding in the yet warm lair of the Rocky Mountain grizzly bear. He sees cities like Omaha, Denver and Leadville sprung, as if by magic, from the silence and nothingness of ten or twenty years ago, into all the rush, bustle, luxury and elegance of metropolitan life, with churches, theatres, hotels, water-works, banks, daily papers, street-cars, electric lights, telephones, and all the conveniences found in the oldest and most wealthy portions of this country and Europe. To him it is like discovering a new continent, and for the first time in his life he realizes how contracted have been his previous ideas regarding the extent, wealth, and grandeur of what is to him a new world in the mighty West.

He finds a country whose resources are as boundless as its limits, and that there is nothing that the eye, heart or imagination can desire, that it does not offer or cannot show.

Here are homes for nations yet unborn, where all riches of soil and mineral, all charms of climate and the beauties of scene unite to frame earth's grandest garden-spot. Here may he dwell on lake or mountain side, in fertile valley or the beautiful plain, in a land of meadows and fruit-trees, of vineyards and golden grain; under the feet a carpet of flowers, and the bluest of heavens bending above and resting its arch on the walls of the forest. The West unrolls before him millions on millions of acres which are to be had for little more than the mere asking or taking.

Does he seek for gold and silver? The greatest mines of earth are yet to be opened in the American Great West. Mountains of golden and silver ore, beside which all the famed riches of the Comstock lode will some day sink to beggars' pence, yet rear their proud heads to heaven, untouched by pick or spade. The veritable treasure-houses of the gods yet await the enterprise and muscle of the sturdy miners, who are destined ere long to fire the avarice and the envy of the world with their Midas-surpassing wealth of solid ducats. The surface dirt of Colorado, Arizona, New Mexico, California, Montana and Idaho mines is hardly broken: the glittering hoards are scarcely touched; the great

Scene at Riverside, suburban town on the
Burlington Route.

bonanza fortunes are yet
to be made.

If he is a lover of the
sublime and beautiful in
natural scenery, the
weird wonders of the

Yellowstone Park and the Garden of the Gods, the mighty cañons of the Yosemite and the Colorado, the majestic peaks of the Rocky Mountains, afford an ever-changing and always glorious feast. It is a realm of mountains and waterfalls, of cloud-wreathed crags, awful chasms, boundless plains, gigantic floods and yawning caverns; a transcendent panorama of all that is sublime and most gorgeous in rugged nature's handiwork; a vast scene from enchanted land, eclipsing all the wonders of oriental fable, hushing the proudest landscape boasts of all the rest of creation, and defying all human genius, with pen or brush or pencil, to depict its grandeur and its loveliness. The sun in heaven, in his grand round, never looked down upon a more glorious realm.

The Colorado tourist as he wanders among its magnificent scenery, can well appreciate the feelings of a well-known and popular poet, who on passing through the Gateway to the Garden of the Gods for the first time, exclaimed as its wonders and beauties burst on his view:

> "Where could our Hearts with more reverence bow,
> What Temple more grand than encircles us now,
> Whose roof is the Heavens, whose floor is the sod,
> Whose walls are the mountains, whose builder is God?"

II.

Six Great States that Form the Heart of the Continent.

In the heart and center of this magnificent domain, itself the heart of the continent, six of the grandest States of the American Union unroll their beauty and riches to the admiring gaze of men. In the exact geographical center of the fairest half of the new world, stretching from the great lakes to the Rocky Mountains, Illinois, Missouri, Iowa, Kansas, Nebraska and Colorado form an empire grander in its resources and capabilities than any emperor or czar, prince or potentate of the older civilizations ever swayed sceptre over. Alexander, when he had conquered the ancient world, ruled no such royal realm. The Cæsars, when Rome's resistless eagles spread their golden wings triumphant from the burning sands of Africa to the mist-clad hills of Caledonia, drew tribute and homage from no such empire. The ambition of Napoleon might have been content with such a domain. Over a thousand miles in length from east to west, and from three to six hundred miles in width from north to south; its eastern shores washed by the blue waves of Lake Michigan, and its western slopes reposing in the shadows of the gold-ribbed giants of the mighty Sierras; traversed for hundreds of miles by America's two greatest rivers, the Mississippi and Missouri, it embraces every variety of soil, and is capable of yielding in exhaustless profusion all the products of the temperate zone. It abounds in wild and romantic scenes, great rivers, boundless prairies and forests, picturesque mountains, incalculable mineral wealth, and pasture-lands on which the cattle of a nation may feed to the full. A brief glance at the six States composing this glorious continental heart and center will not be unprofitable.

ILLINOIS.

Among the great States of the West, Illinois stands first.   The
name is derived from the Indian word, *Illini*, signifying "Superior
Men," and the early French gave it a termination to suit their
tongue.   The five tribes constituting the Illinois confederation were the Peorias, Cahokas, Tamaroras, Kaskaskias and

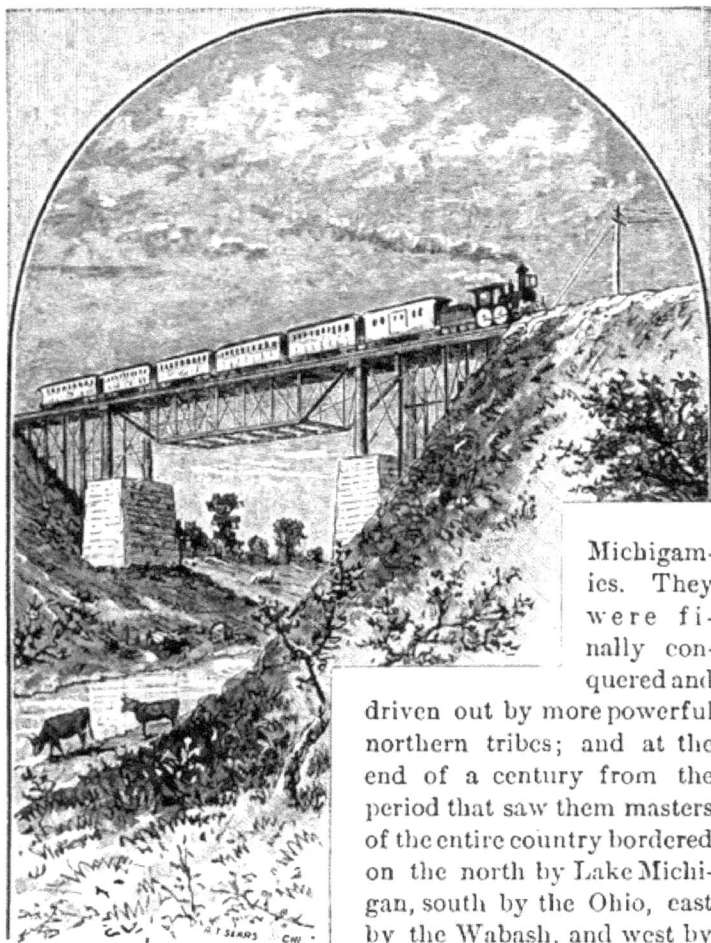

Michigam-
ies.   They
w e r e fi-
nally con-
quered and
driven out by more powerful
northern tribes; and at the
end of a century from the
period that saw them masters
of the entire country bordered
on the north by Lake Michigan, south by the Ohio, east
by the Wabash, and west by
the Mississippi, not a vestige of

Bridge across Bureau Creek, Ill., on the line of
the Chicago, Burlington & Quincy R. R.

their former greatness remained, and the few surviving members of the once proud and powerful Illinois confederation had been absorbed by other tribes from whom they sought protection from their relentless northern foes. The first white settlements were made by the French. Nicholas Perrot in 1671 was probably the first white man who ever visited the region, followed by Joliet and Marquette in 1673. In 1679, La Salle descended the Illinois river, and built a small fort, which he named Crèvecœur, at the foot of Peoria lake. In 1682, he made a second trip from Canada, bringing a considerable colony with him, and establishing settlements at Kaskaskia, Cahokia and other places. In 1778 the government of Virginia sent Lieutenant-Colonel George Rogers Clark, than whom a braver or better officer never unfurled the American flag, to conquer the British garrisons in the West, and in July of that year Kaskaskia, then the capital of Illinois, was captured, and shortly after the fort at Crèvecœur, near Peoria, and the British then evacuated the Territory. In the succeeding month of October, Virginia erected the whole conquered country, embracing all the territory west of the Ohio river, into the County of Illinois. In 1784 Virginia ceded all this territory to the United States. In February, 1790, St. Clair County (the first county in the State) was organized, with Kaskaskia as the county seat. On May 7th, 1800, the Territory of Indiana was carved out of the Territory of the Northwest, and embraced the present States of Indiana, Illinois, Michigan and Wisconsin. On the third of February, 1809, the Territory of Illinois was detached from the Territory of Indiana, and constituted a separate Territory, having then a population estimated at 9,000. Kaskaskia was the first seat of government. The 3d of December, 1818, Illinois was admitted as a State of the Union, with a population of 45,000. By the census of 1820 it had 55,211; in 1850, 851,470; in 1870, 2,539,891; and 3,077,771 in 1880. Since then its growth has kept pace with any previous period.

The State is three hundred and eighty miles long, with an average width of a hundred and fifty-six miles, and an area of 55,414 square miles, or 35,465,093 acres, ninety per cent. of which is tillable land. It is mostly a high table land, of prairie and timber beautifully intermingled, with an elevation of from four to eight hundred feet above the level of the sea. Its soil is inexhaustibly fertile, and nowhere on earth do the labors of the husbandman yield richer returns. Illinois farmers are universally thrifty and independent. A large part of the State is like a vast garden; neat houses, fine barns, blooming orchards, tasteful hedges, broad fields of golden grain, meadows and vineyards, and green pastures dotted with flocks and herds of thoroughbred cattle, sheep, horses and other stock, forming a continuous panorama of agricultural beauty and prosperity. Half its hundred and two county-seats are cities of commercial and financial importance, Chicago, its commercial metropolis, being the fourth city in the Union in population, the second in commerce, and the first in enterprise and promise. Every branch of manufacturing is carried on in the State, and stock-raising is an extensive and profitable industry. In the production of wheat, corn and oats, Illinois is the first State in the Union; in live stock, second; in rye, third; in value of manufactures and amount of capital employed, sixth; of distilled liquors, dressed lumber and packed provisions, first. The coal fields of Illinois cover an area of 45,000 square miles. The coal is bituminous, well adapted for steam and domestic purposes, and is extensively used by iron manufacturers. The production in 1880 was 4,000,000 tons, and was only exceeded in the extent of its output by Pennsylvania and Ohio.

The following shows the leading articles of farm products and live stock produced by Illinois in 1880, as shown by the assessors' returns:

Wheat, bushels 60,958,757	Irish Potatoes, bushels ..6,470,811
Corn, bushels..........252,697,896	Pounds of Butter sold..24,553,449
Oats, bushels...........62,946,510	Pounds of Cheese sold...6,187,680
Rye, bushels.............3,049,860	Cows kept, number........613,728
Barley, bushels..........1,109,245	Cattle, total No. in State.1,999,788
Flax Seed, bushels 1,557,898	Cattle, No. marketed 2,473,727
Timothy Seed, bushels....400,124	Hogs, total No. in State..3,133,557
Clover Seed, bushels 87,144	Hogs, No. marketed......2,642,606
Other Grass Seeds, bushels, 66,789	Sheep, total No. in State ..964,696
Tobacco, lbs............2,736,406	Sheep, No. marketed......193,384
Broom Corn, lbs........14,457,156	Horses, number..........912,586
Hay, tons marketed......3,486,584	Mules and Asses, number..116,260

Its railroad system is the finest in the Union; its whole surface being checkered with the iron pathways of trade and travel. The State has within its limits 1,300 miles of navigable river, Lake Michigan washes its northern frontier, and the Illinois and Michigan canal connects the great lakes with the Illinois and Mississippi rivers, affording every facility of trans-

View in Springdale, Peoria, Ill.

portation. The assessed valuation of the State in 1880 was $799,813,566. Religious and educational institutions abound everywhere and are well supported. The State has lavishly provided for all its unfortunates. There are three insane asylums, one deaf and dumb asylum, one asylum for the blind, one for the education of feeble-minded children, one charitable eye and ear infirmary, and an admirably managed home for soldiers' orphans. Some of these institutions are on a magnificent scale. The penitentiary is at Joliet, and a branch at Chester. In addition to the

State normal university at Normal, and its southern branch at Carbondale, there are the Illinois industrial university at Urbana, and the Illinois agricultural school at Irvington, besides some thirty colleges, forty academies, law and medical schools, theological seminaries, and six hundred or more high grade private schools and seminaries. The State, under the new apportionment, has twenty representatives in Congress, and at its present rate of growth bids fair to be, ere long, second only to New York, if not even to her.

IOWA.

Just west of the northern portion of Illinois and the southern part of Wisconsin lies the second great State of the six that form the heart of the continent. Iowa, as its name in the Indian tongue denotes, is a "Beautiful Land." On all the globe there is none, as an agricultural region, a home-land, more beautiful or more bountiful. It is three hundred miles long from east to west and two hundred wide from north to south, and contains an area of 55,045 square miles or 35,288,800 acres, almost exactly the same as Illinois. Its shores are washed for three hundred and sixty-five miles on the east by the Mississippi river, and for three hundred and sixty-four miles on the west by the Missouri, making a total of seven hundred and twenty-nine miles of frontage on the two greatest rivers of North America. Thousands of small streams traverse every portion of the State, furnishing drainage and abundant water-supply, and in the northern counties there are hundreds of crystal lakes swarming with delicious fish. The whole surface of the State is beautifully undulating prairie, interspersed along all the streams with groves of oak, elm, walnut, ash, hickory, maple, linn and cottonwood. Living springs burst from the hillsides everywhere. The climate is delightful, healthful and invigorating, ranking according to the census statistics among the first in salubrity. There are few swamps or stagnate sloughs, no miasma or malaria, and nothing conducive to disease. Pulmonary complaints are scarcely known. The soil of Iowa has become famous throughout the world for its fertility. Ninety-five hundredths of the entire surface of the State is tillable land, and it is not surpassed in productiveness by that of any other region, in the United States. Reliable statisticians declare that the wonderful soil of this State alone is capable of a cultivation that would yield harvests amply sufficient to feed 40,000,000 people. Corn is a specially profitable crop, yielding from thirty to seventy-five bushels to the acre. Wheat and oats do well in all parts of the State. Flax is also raised with great success All root crops yield well. Wild and tame grasses and clover grow luxuriantly everywhere. Stock-raising is rapidly becoming a great and profitable industry. Abundance of nutritious grass, plenty of pure water, ample timber for shade, and the fullest facilities of rail and water transportation to reach the markets, ensure success to any stock-grower of ordinary intelligence and energy. Iowa, though one of the youngest States in the Union, already ranks first as a producer of hogs, and second in corn. Fruit-growing is successfully and extensively prosecuted. Iowa has for years taken the first premiums at the national horticultural exhibitions for the finest apples, and the greatest number and varieties. The coal-fields of Iowa cover an area of over 20,000 square miles, and mining is successfully carried on in some thirty-five different counties. The coal is bituminous, and of fair quality. Large amounts of capital are being invested, and large numbers of workmen employed, in coal-mining, and the industry is rapidly growing. This, with abundant and constantly increasing facilities of railroad transportation, added to the supply of wood from the groves and forests that dot all the State, ensures ample and cheap fuel for all private and public uses. Gypsum of the finest quality exists in exhaustless deposits. Limestone, suitable for making first-class quicklime, is plenty in most parts of the State, and excellent building stone is quarried in a majority of the ninety-nine counties into which the State is sub-divided. Lead has, for years, been extensively mined, while potters' clay, fire clay and clay suitable for brick-making abound, and valuable deposits of mineral paint have lately been discovered in several places. Peat has been found in some of the northern counties, but has not been much used. The great national highway across the continent lies directly through Southern Iowa, and her railroad system is a vast and swiftly growing one. In 1860, twenty States had more lines of railway; now there are but four. This progress in railroad construction shows the confidence of capitalists in the future of the State. Every part of the State is traversed by the iron tracks of progress, and the work of building additional lines goes ceaselessly on. Churches, schools and all the varieties of educational,

ENTRANCE TO FAIR GROUNDS

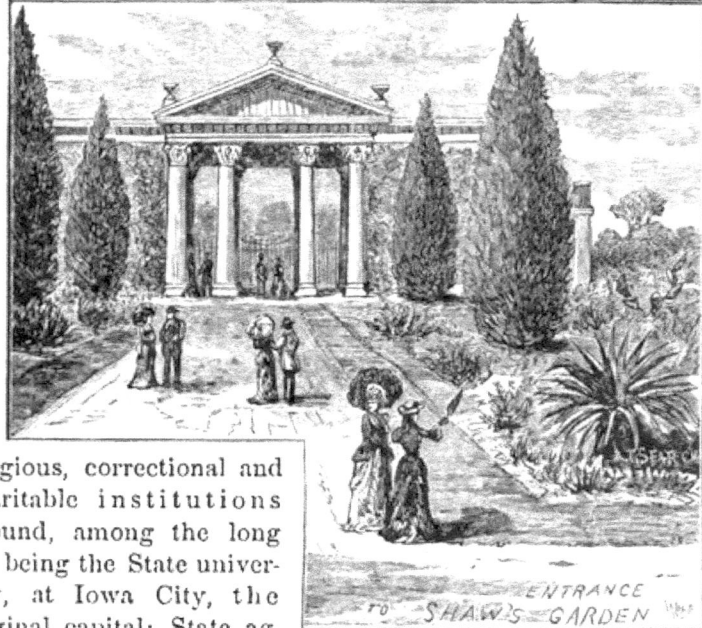

ENTRANCE TO SHAW'S GARDEN

St. Louis, Missouri.

religious, correctional and charitable institutions abound, among the long list being the State university, at Iowa City, the original capital; State agricultural college and model farm, at Ames; training school for teachers, at Cedar Falls; institution for the support of the deaf and dumb, at Council Bluffs; college for the blind, at Vinton; home for soldiers' orphans and home for indigent children, at Davenport; asylum for feeble-minded children, at Glenwood; State reform school for boys, at Eldora; State reform school for girls, at Mitchellville; hospitals for the insane, at Mount Pleasant and Independence; State penitentiary, at Fort Madison, and additional penitentiary at Anamosa. The educational system of the State ranks among the best in the Union. There are over 12,000 school-houses, and the annual expenditure for public school purposes is upwards of $5,000,000, a portion of which is derived from the school lands. Besides this there are many denominational colleges and high grade schools, and the official statistics of the United States census show fewer illiterate people in proportion to population in Iowa than in any other State of the Union. Newspapers abound and are well supported everywhere. When Iowa was admitted into the Union in 1846, its population was but little over 100,000. The census of 1850 gave it a population of 192,214; that of 1860 showed 674,913, an increase during the decade of more than three hundred per cent.; that of 1870 footed up 1,194,020, a growth during the ten years of nearly a hundred per cent.; and the last census, that of 1880, showed a population of 1,624,620, which has before this time swelled to over 1,800,000. Since 1860, the percentage of increase has been four times that of the United States at large. Nine States, that outranked Iowa in population in 1870, now stand below it. Of the 35,228,800 acres of land in Iowa, scarcely one-half has yet been brought into even nominal cultivation, and the unimproved lands are equal in fertility to any in the State. The railroad companies are offering their lands for sale at from three to fifteen dollars an acre, and large tracts held by private parties in nearly every county are being placed in market at low prices. In some parts of the State excellent lands can be obtained at from four to ten dollars. With such lands to be had almost for the asking, in a State that has no debt and where taxation is scarcely more than nominal, where the soil and climate are unsurpassed, with water and fuel in abundance, limitless facilities of transportation to the markets of the world, among an intelligent and hospitable population, blessed with all possible educational advantages, what region on earth can offer more inducements to the seeker for a home? And, with inexhaustible supplies of raw material, coal for fuel, stone and wood for building, and water-power for running machinery, what State in all the Union presents more opportunities to the manufacturer and enterprising capitalist, than Iowa?

The dairy interest of Iowa is developing with wonderful rapidity. Colonel Littler, secretary of the National Dairymen's Association, says that ten years ago there was not a regular creamery in the State; now there are 500, with an annual product of 85,000,000 lbs. of butter, 50 per cent. of which is shipped out of the State, netting a profit of $10,000,000, to which he says may be added over $2,000,000 for cheese, after supplying the home demand. Iowa butter took the first premium at the Centennial Exhibition in 1876, and its general rank is equal to the best produced in the United States. A single sale to an English buyer last year amounted to $40,000. The shipment went direct to London.

As an evidence that the Chicago, Burlington & Quincy Railroad traverses the most productive portions of this enormously prolific State, a compilation has been made from the report of the Iowa railroad commissioners showing the total production of the leading articles, and the channels through which the surplus was shipped east from the State in 1880:

	Amount Produced.	Moved by C. B. & Q. R. R.	Total moved by all other lines.
Corn, bu..........	230,633,200	26,199,018	51,908,751
Wheat, bu............	36,099,769	5,333,423	9,305,519
Oats, bu.............	41,288,800	4,555,285	12,170,187
Rye, bu..............	574,000	383,018	757,516
Barley, bu............	4,600,000	783,755	1,770,710
Potatoes, bu..........	10,165,000	1,764,000	1,959,000
Cattle, No............	2,612,006	210,630	410,139
Hogs, No.............	2,778,400	989,499	2,241,841
Sheep, No............	463,488	21,838	47,274

MISSOURI.

Almost in the exact geographical center of the United States, an empire in proportions, a paradise in beauty, and a treasure-house of the genii and fairies in natural resources, lies the great State of Missouri. Two hundred and eighty-two miles in length from north to south, and three hundred and forty-eight miles in breadth from east to west, the State has an area of 65,350 square

View at Burlington, Iowa, from Third Street Hill.

miles, or 41,824,000 acres. It is eight times as large as Massachusetts, and ranks as the eighth in the Union in size. Lying as it does on the exact line where the happy medium is found in climate, it escapes the rigors of the far northern winters and the torrid heats of far southern summers, while its vast extent and diversified surface afford every variety of temperate climate. Its soil is capable of producing almost every grain, grass, fruit, and timber of the temperate zones. It raised in 1880, 160,000,000 bushels of corn, 29,563,000 bushels of wheat, 300,000 bushels of flax-seed, 20,000,000 pounds of tobacco. While the portion of the State north of the Missouri river is second to none for the production of grain and grasses, that laying south is especially adapted to fruit. Grapes are extensively cultivated for table purposes and wine making, and there are few wines that rank superior to those made from Missouri grapes. Although this industry is still in its infancy, those who are most competent to judge, express the opinion that ere the end of the present century the vineyards of Missouri will alone give employment to tens of thousands of people, and the production of wines become one of its leading industries. Cotton is also largely grown in the southern counties. Vast forests of valuable cypress, oak, elm, poplar, hickory, ash, walnut, maple, cedar and pine are found in the southern portion. The mineral wealth of the State is unsurpassed perhaps by that of any region of similar area on the globe. The great Iron Mountain has long been one of the wonders of the world to tourists and scientists. The lead mines of Missouri are among the richest in the world. There are 26,000 square miles of coal lands in the State, and the supply is ample to meet all the demands of the State for generations to come. Copper, zinc, cobalt, manganese, nickel, gypsum, baryta, kaolin, marble, onyx and granite, are found in many portions of the State, but chiefly in the southern part.

The Mississippi river washes the eastern border of the State for 450 miles; and the Missouri, after forming its western boundary for two hundred and fifty miles, turns to the east and flows almost through the centre of the State four hundred miles to its junction with the Mississippi. The Osage, Gasconade and Lamine rivers are all navigable, and thousands of smaller streams furnish every part of the State with a never-failing supply of pure water. All these streams abound with delicious fish. All over the State springs of water clear as crystal gush from the hillsides. One of these, called Bryce's spring, on the Niangua, in southwestern Missouri, is said to discharge 10,000,000 cubic feet of water a day, and in many instances mills are run by water-power furnished by these remarkable fountains. In the vast comparatively unsettled regions of the State game is abundant. Missouri is divided into a hundred and fifteen counties, and has a population of 2,169,000. It contains over 1,500 cities and villages, 150,000 cultivated farms, 17,000 manufacturing establishments, 4,000 miles of railroad, 1,600 post-offices, over 10,000 public schools and 2,000 private schools, two hundred collegiate institutions, and has an educational fund of nearly $7,500,000. It employs $125,000,000 of manufacturing capital, paying out yearly for wages and material $210,000,000, and producing $275,000,000 in manufactured goods. The timber, coal, iron, lead, copper and zinc, the cotton, flax and wool, and the magnificent water-power to be found almost everywhere, hold out unsurpassed inducements to enterprising capitalists and manufacturers. The vast areas of rich lands, as yet unbroken by plow or harrow and for sale at low prices; the infinite variety of productions, the delightful climate, the healthfulness, the exhaustless supplies of timber, coal and building stone, the abundance of pure spring water and the ample educational advantages of Missouri, particularly the north-western portion, unite to render it a veritable Canaan, a land of promise and rich fulfilment, to the seeker for a home.

KANSAS.

No State has cut a more important figure in the history of the Union than Kansas, and few, if any, have made greater advancement in population, and all that tends to material wealth. The cause of its almost unparalleled prosperity is due to its delightful climate and fertile soil. The settler had but to select his home, sow and reap. So easily was the soil brought under cultivation, that tens of thousands of acres that were clothed with rich and beautiful autumnal flora in September, waved with golden grain the following July. Being in the great pathway across the continent, the railroads did not wait for the settler, but preceded him, hence the latter was provided with ready means for transportation ere he had such patronage to bestow.

The act organizing the territory was passed May 30, 1854, and Kansas was admitted as a State January 29, 1861. In 1860 the population was 107,206; in 1870 it was 364,339; in 1880, 995,966, and is now estimated at 1,250,000,

Kansas has an area of 81,318 square miles, or 52,043,520 acres, of land as beautiful and fertile as ever a crow flew over. In 1866 Kansas was the twenty-fourth State in the Union in agricultural products; in 1878, just twelve years later, it surpassed every other State but four in its wheat yield, and

View of Keokuk, Iowa.

stood fourth in corn. Its corn crop in 1868 was 24,500,000 bushels; and in 1879 it had risen to 105,729,927 bushels, an increase of four hundred and fifty per cent. in eleven years. Such rapidity of development has never been paralleled in the history of the world, except perhaps in Nebraska alone.

Of the 52,043,520 acres of land within the limits of Kansas, scarcely 11,000,000 are as yet in cultivation. Vast tracts of as beautiful land as human eye ever beheld, still lie awaiting the coming of the sturdy husbandman and herdsman. The western part of the State, on the headwaters of the Kansas and Arkansas rivers, is one vast open pasture of thousands of square miles, where millions of cattle and sheep can be grazed the whole year round. The grass grows from one to six feet in height all over these mighty pampas, where scarcely more than ten years ago countless herds of buffalo found rich subsistence, summer and

Grave of the celebrated Indian Chief Black Hawk, near Keokuk, Iowa.

winter. With a few hundred dollars invested in sheep or cattle, any young man of energy and ordinary industry and judgment can make himself independent in this region in a few years. In addition to the magnificent grain and grass crops, fruit and melons of all kinds do well, grapes reach the highest degree of perfection, and potatoes and other root crops and garden vegetables grow to an enormous size and yield immensely. All the world beheld with amazement the grain, grass, fruit and vegetable display made by Kansas at the Centennial Exposition in Philadelphia in 1876, which excited wide-spread interest in the young giant State from which it came. The southeastern part of the State is underlaid by an almost unbroken coal-bed and mining is carried on extensively and profitably. Fine water-power is afforded by many of the streams. Salt springs abound in the valleys of the Republican, Solomon and Saline rivers, and at one place in the western part of the State there is a vast bed of crystallized salt varying from six inches to upward of two feet in thickness. Lead, alum, zinc, mineral paints, limestone suitable for hydraulic cement, and many varieties of excellent building stone are found in different portions of the State. Unimproved lands can be bought at low prices even in the most thickly settled portions of the State, and further west there are still homes for hundreds of thousands at government rates. The tide of immigration is pouring in from every part of the world. The most unquestionable evidence of its rapid and substantial prosperity is shown by the fact that in 1874 the total assessed value of live stock of all kinds and farm products was $39,374,153.80, and in 1881, $122,946,489.95, showing an increase of $83,572,336.15. The real value of property of all kinds per capita, in 1881, was $440.31. Increase in the land cultivated in 1881 over 1874 was 6,125,300 acres. Increase in cultivated land in 1882 over 1881, 1,192,163 acres. The following shows the yield of the principal farm products for the year 1881: Wheat, 19,909,000 bu.; corn, 80,760,000 bu.; oats, 8,754,000 bu.; rye, 467,000 bu.; barley, 243,000 bu.; buckwheat, 58,621 bu.; flaxseed, 1,184,445 bu.; broom corn, 32,961,150 lbs.; castor beans, 392,549 bu.; Irish potatoes, 1,854,140 bu. The corn crop this year is estimated at 175,100,000 bu., and the wheat at 36,000,000 bu.

NEBRASKA.

Youngest but one of all the States in the Union, it is claimed for Nebraska that it surpasses all the others in comparative rapidity of development, capacity of production and all the advan-

tages and inducements that govern the choice of seekers for
homes and fortunes in the west. In growth, Kansas alone of all
the States has ever rivaled it. In 1855, its population was 4,494;
and in 1880, it was 452,542, having multiplied over a hundred-fold
in twenty-five years. In 1860, its population was 28,481, six times
what it was five years before. In 1870, it had increased to 122,993,
nearly five-fold in ten years; and in the ten years following,
the increase was nearly four-fold. The population of the State
is now estimated at fully 600,000. Four States claim to be the
exact geographical center of the republic, Missouri, Iowa, Kansas
and Nebraska, and the last is far from least. The State has an area
of 76,000 square miles, or 48,640,000 acres, of which nearly every
acre is valuable for tillage or pasture. With a population as dense
as that of Ohio, seventy-five to the square mile, Nebraska would
maintain 5,700,000 people. With two hundred and thirty to the
square mile, as in Massachusetts, Nebraska would be an empire
of 17,480,000 souls. The taxable values of the State in 1870
were $53,709,828, and in 1880 they were $90,431,757, an increase
of nearly seventy per cent. The annual increase in the value of
lands is from ten to twenty per cent. It is but a few years since
the whistle of the first locomotive was heard within the borders
of the State. Now it has nearly 3,000 miles of railroad. The
State is abundantly supplied with schools, colleges and all the
varieties of charitable, educational and reformatory institutions.
Its common school system is based upon a land grant of 2,443,148
acres, which will yield a fund of over $18,000,000. The grain
product of the State in 1874 was 10,000,000 bushels; in 1879, it
was 100,000,000 bushels, a ten-fold increase in five years, or two
hundred per cent. each year. In 1878, the State produced 295,000
head of hogs, and in 1879, 700,000, an increase of nearly two
hundred and fifty per cent. in a single year. It annually
raises over 300,000 cattle and 250,000 sheep. The climate cannot
be surpassed for healthfulness and all invigorating qualities. The
pure and bracing air is the surest tonic for invalids suffering from
malarial, catarrhal or bronchial troubles. The perfect clearness
of the atmosphere is one of the things that strikes every stranger,
enabling one to distinguish objects at double or treble the distance that is possible in less favored regions. The whole State is

magnificently watered, and dotted with groves of timber. It is favorably situated between the fortieth and forty-third degrees of north latitude, where all climatic vigor and mildness meet, and in the very belt upon the surface of the globe which has in all ages

Rail Road Bridge across Skunk River, near Rome, Iowa.

produced the highest type of men and women, the highest development, physical, intellectual and moral. The surface of the State is like a vast stretch of landscape gardening, gently undulating prairies interspersed with groves of timber and diversified by numberless streams of pure water. The soil is a rich black loam, being in many places from two to twenty feet in depth, underlaid by a stiff clay, and remarkable for its ability to produce good crops in the dryest season. From forty to eighty bushels of corn to the acre is not an unusual crop in the valleys, and from eighteen to twenty-five bushels of wheat may be relied upon as the yield under any favorable circumstances. Apples, pears, plums, cherries and all the fruits common in this latitude, yield abundantly and of the finest quality. Garden vegetables, potatoes, onions, turnips and melons of all kinds give immense returns for slight cultivation.

The purity of its atmosphere, and excellence of its tame and wild grasses, especially adapt the State, particularly the southeastern portion, to dairy purposes, and although this branch of farm industry is in its infancy, it is rapidly developing. According to the census returns of 1880 there were 161,787 milch cows in the State, and the number has largely increased since that period.

The western part of the State is the stock-grower's paradise. On the vast plains that stretch from the Republican river to the Niobrara, across the valleys of the Platte, Middle and North Fork of the Loup, the Elkhorn and the Snake rivers, the cattle of a great nation might feed. The grass grows in rank luxuriance, in many places along the streams that everywhere diversify the surface attaining a height so great that a man on horseback can scarcely see over it. Little care is necessary the year round, and the ratio of increase of a herd is almost beyond belief. Cattle and sheep enjoy entire immunity from the diseases which ravage the flocks and herds of nearly every other region, and the expense of rearing them is literally almost nothing. In the most beautiful and fertile portions of the State, the grand valleys of the Platte and Republican rivers, the Burlington & Missouri River Railroad Company, a part of the great Chicago, Burlington & Quincy Railroad system, has 500,000 acres of splendid lands for sale at from two to ten dollars an acre, on long credit and most favorable terms to buyers. In the western part of the State, where settlements are as yet comparatively few and far between, millions of acres still remain subject to entry as homesteads, pre-emptions or timber claims under the government land laws. Of all the magnificent group of States, that form the subject of this brief treatise, none possesses more advantages or offers more inducements to the seeker for a home and a fortune. A soil as fertile as the far-famed valley of the Nile, and a climate as healthful as ever was fanned by the pure airs of primeval paradise. Timber, water, limitless capacities of production. Boundless ranges for flocks and herds. In the language of Holy Writ, "A land of brooks and water, of fountains and depths that spring out of valleys and hills; a land of wheat and barley; a land wherein thou shalt eat bread without scarceness; thou shalt not lack anything in it." With all these riches of resources and charms, with as fine religious and educational advantages as any region of the world, with an intelligent, moral and enterprising population, and with 20,000,000 acres to be had for little more than a song, it is easy to understand the magnificent growth of the State. It is no wonder that untold thousands of strong-armed and clear-headed immigrants, the brain and brawn that build states and empires, are pouring in like a ceaseless, ever-swelling tide from every region of our own country and of the world. The next census will find Nebraska in population, wealth and all the elements of power far ahead of many States that enjoyed a half century of culture and development before the great Nebraskan wilderness was broken by a white settlement. The whole State is dotted with universities, colleges, schools and churches. Its population is noted throughout the republic, as conspicuous, even among the brainy and pushing people of the American Great West, for intelligence, enterprise and untiring vigor of body and mind, honesty and a high degree of culture and refinement.

COLORADO.

Colorado is the youngest State in the Union, having been admitted in 1876, on the nation's centennial anniversary. But although the youngest in years, it is a lusty youth, and in natural resources, delightfulness of climate, beauty and grandeur of scenery, it has no equal among the older members of the family that constitute the American Union of States. Its history renders tame the tales of the Arabian Nights, and makes all fables and fairy stories seem commonplace and probable. All gorgeous legends and romances have found full realization here. The wildest dreams of oriental poets and romancers, all the weird, resplendent creations of magi and genii, become waking facts amid these miracle-wrought crags and cañons. All the sublimest glories of the Swiss and Italian Alps, all the picturesque savagery of the Tyrol, and all the softer beauties of Killarney and Como and Naples dwindle to insignificance by comparison with the stupendous scenes that meet the gaze at every turn in Colorado : vast peaks, whose crowns of everlasting snow and ice glitter in the

View on line of C., B. & Q. R. R., near Ottumwa, Iowa.

sunlight far above where storms and torrents roar; chasms so profound that their yawning depths seem glimpses of the bottomless caverns where plutonian shadows walk and Titans strive; cataracts, whose crystal floods dissolve to snowy foam and spray long before they strike the rocky basins' dizzy distances below. It is a land of giant crags and fathomless abysses, carved by unending ages of whirlpools and eddies ; a land of cloud-wreathed heights and awful depths, of whirling waters, of rocks and tumbling streams and flying spray. Rainbows cast their glittering coronets around the mountains' lofty brows, and radiant irises dance in many a romantic gorge Colorado is Fairyland, a region where elves and gnomes might sport and make their homes. Among all the regions of earth, it is pre-eminently the tourist's paradise, the holy land of sight-seers and lovers of Nature in her sublimest and loveliest moods. It is the great world's sanitarium. Amid these inspiring scenes the air is dry and pure as that which fanned the cheek of sinlessness in primal Eden. Catarrh, hay-fever and asthma vanish at once beneath its balmy influence. Even tubercular consumption finds relief and often cure. From the strange Deity-wrought laboratories of the mountain-sides all over the State, burst forth the magical fountains of healing for invalids of every class. Every variety of medicinal waters known to humanity is found somewhere in this Wonderland. Hot springs that possess all the virtues of the Arkansas Springs are found in nearly a score of different places, and their waters are a sure relief for rheumatism, gout, dyspepsia, and almost every form of nervous, inflammatory and cutaneous disease. Sulphur springs of every known variety— white, red, yellow and black, hot and cold—are found in many different places, as well as soda, magnesia, and all the countless species of chalybeate springs. The sick and enfeebled of every land may here find some specific, compounded by Jehovah's own all-wise hand, for their relief or cure, and thousands who first went to Colorado by prescription of physicians, scarcely hoping to find temporary alleviation of the tortures of disease, now live in vigorous rejuvenation to sound the praises of the grand region which is destined to be the greatest health resort of the world.

Colorado has an area of 104,500 square miles, nearly as large as all the New England States and New York combined. Its mountain-sides are covered with forests of valuable timber, and are swollen with their hidden wealth of gold and silver, iron, copper, lead and coal. All the valleys and foothills are covered with a luxuriant growth of nutritious grass, and the soil when properly irrigated yields rich returns for the husbandman's labor. Streams of water pure as ever flowed from the distilleries of the skies ripple and tumble through the cañons, furnishing water-power enough to turn all the world's machinery The State contains at least 5,000,000 acres of tillable land, of which little over 120,000 acres are in cultivation; and yet the yield in 1880 was 1,425,014 bushels of wheat, 640,900 bushels of oats, 455,968 bushels of corn, 107,116 bushels of barley, besides large crops of all kinds of garden products. As a grazing region Colorado offers many advantages, the grass affording abundant food nearly all the year, and the mildness of the climate and the protection of the timber-clad mountains rendering shelter almost unnecessary. The business of stock-raising in the State is yet in its infancy, but the value of the herds is about $16,000,000, and the sales for last year were $1,500,000 more than for the year before. There is literally no expense about raising cattle except the pay of herders, and nearly all that is received from sales is clear profit. Counting interest on capital, the Colorado stockman expects to average a profit of from twenty to fifty per cent. a year. Sheep-raising is even more sure and profitable, as they increase more rapidly. But the great industry of Colorado, that which has made this six-year-old State the gathering-place of capitalists and fortune-seekers from every land beneath the sun, that which has made its name a talismanic word throughout the world, is its marvelous mines of gold and silver. They are the wonder of mankind. They have eclipsed the dazzling miracles of Aladdin and his lamp. They have enabled the rude day-laborers of ten or fifteen years ago to vie with the Rothschilds, and to surpass kings and emperors, in the colossal proportions of their fortunes. They have empowered the raw grocer's clerk of 1877 to astonish a continent with the magnificence of his architectural creations in 1881. They have turned the heads of the world, and enabled the children of this generation to smile at the most gorgeous fairy-tales that amazed their fathers and mothers, as trivial and tame, when they can rub daily against the jewel-clad creatures of infinitely more marvelous stories in real life. Colorado leads all the world as a producer of gold and silver. The names of Denver, Leadville, Georgetown, Silver Cliff, Gunnison, Boulder and a score of other wild Colorado mining-camps, many of which were undreamt of ten or fifteen years ago, are as well and widely known as New York, Paris, London or Rome. In twenty-three years the State has yielded $140,584,752 of gold and silver bullion. Last year the yield was $23,687,685, or about one-third of the total product of the United States, and an increase of nearly $7,000,000 over the yield of 1879.

And yet, with all this vast production, the crust of its wealth is hardly broken, the surface dirt of its vast deposits of precious metal is scarcely scraped off. Thousands of square miles of moun-

View near Chillicothe, Iowa.

tain-side and gulch are yet to be prospected. Hundreds of mines, that shall some day make all that now are known seem small by comparison, have never yet been touched by miner's pick. The great mining fortunes of the world are yet unmade.

No region on all the beauteous globe offers more attractions or presents more opportunities to the nature-lover, the artist, the tourist, the capitalist, the man of nerve and enterprise, or the invalid, to the seeker for recreation, health or fortune, than Colorado, the Centennial State, the gold-and-jewel-decked queen of the Rockies.

THE SIX GREAT STATES AND THEIR PRODUCTS.

The best evidence of a country's productiveness is the surplus which it sends to market. In order to show that the claim that the Chicago, Burlington & Quincy railroad traverses the most fertile section of the West, North and Southwest, is not based on mere empty assertion, we have compiled from the report of the Chicago Board of Trade, a table showing the receipts of a few leading articles at Chicago for 1880, and the channels through which they were received:

	By the C. B. & Q. R. R.	*By all other Routes.
Wheat, bushels	6,922,638	16,618,969
Corn, bushels.....	40,920,000	36,343,000
Oats, bushels	7,978,000	15,513,000
Rye, bushels..........	527,000	1,342,000
Cattle, number.........	425,371	957,106
Hogs, number	2,156,432	4,992,025
Sheep, number.	60,222	295,589
Provisions, pounds	51,715,000	112,722,000
Lard, pounds......	24,705,000	43,682,000
Wool, pounds	18,034,000	22,162,000
Hides, pounds....	14,773,000	58,351,000

*All other routes included 13 railroads, lake and canal.

The shipments of lumber and shingles from Chicago for the year 1880, were 875,150,000 feet of lumber, of which the C B. & Q. R. R. carried 349,359,000 feet ; and of shingles 110,866,000, of which the C. B. & Q R. R. carried 71,045,000.

It is scarcely deemed necessary to cite further evidence of the unsurpassed productiveness of the States penetrated in all directions by the railroads embraced in the Chicago, Burlington & Quincy system, than is furnished by the above figures; but for the purpose of conveying a more perfect idea as to the position which they occupy toward the remaining thirty-three States and eight Territories within the Union, a statement has been carefully compiled which exhibits the total yield of wheat, corn and oats, with the number of cattle and hogs in the United States and Territories in 1880, together with the proportion produced by the five great States of Illinois, Iowa, Missouri, Kansas and Nebraska. The comparative figures are as follows:

	Wheat, bu	Corn, bu.	Oats, bu.	Cattle, No.	Hogs, No.
Illinois..........	60,959,000	252,697,000	62,947,000	2,384,332	3,202,000
Iowa.............	33,178,000	260,193,000	49,922,000	2,612,006	2,778,400
Missouri....... .	29,563,000	160,463,000	25,314,000	2,080,932	2,020,000
Kansas..........	20,336,000	106,218,000	8,583,000	1,441,557	1,785,000
Nebraska	12,922,000	59,508,000	5,584,000	858,552	1,320,000
Totals...........	156,958,000	849,079,000	152,350,000	9,377,379	11,105,400
Total U. S. 1880..	498,550,000	1,717,435,000	417,885,000	36,093,854	36,247,603

It will be seen by the preceding table, that the States named produced about one-third of the wheat, nearly one-half of the corn, over one-third of the oats and cattle, and nearly thirty-two per cent. of the hogs.

DEBT AND TAXATION.

The State, county and municipal indebtedness of the country traversed by the Chicago, Burlington & Quincy railroad system is lower, in proportion to the wealth and population, than in any

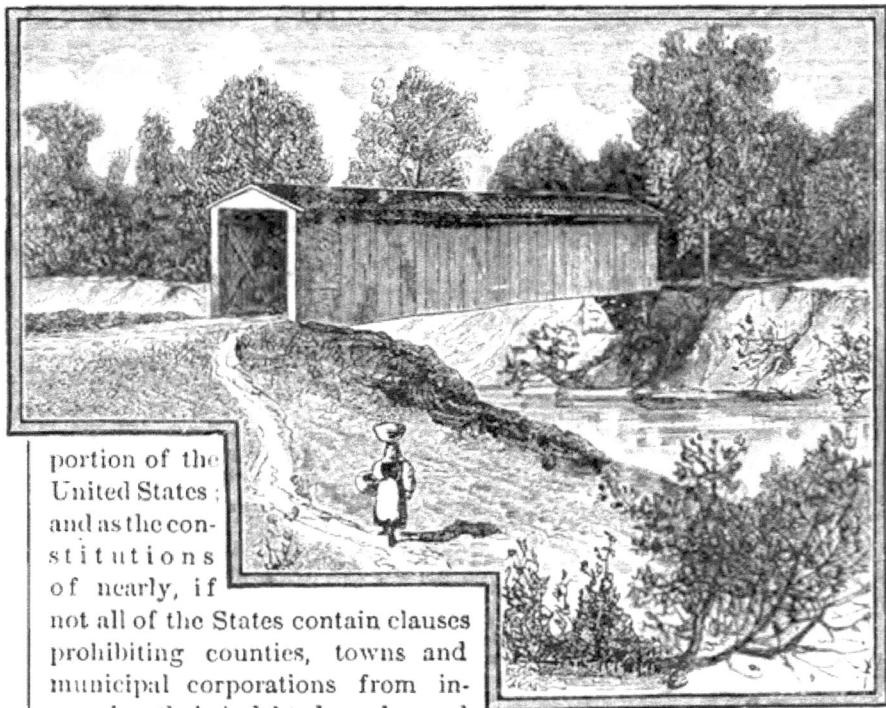

View near Villisca, Iowa.

portion of the United States ; and as the constitutions of nearly, if not all of the States contain clauses prohibiting counties, towns and municipal corporations from increasing their indebtedness beyond very moderate limits, the taxes will continue to decrease, rather than grow, with the expansion of the resources of the country ; hence the immigrant need not fear that his substance will be absorbed by the tax gatherer, as is the case in many other sections of the country.

III.

The Heart's Great Artery of Trade and Travel.

Such is The Heart of the Continent; six glorious hearts, and every heart a queenly State, all grouped in one majestic heart of hearts. It is a realm of infinite resources and beauty, a land of health and plenty and illimitable capacities, in which a hundred millions of prosperous and happy people will some day, and that not far in the future, find homes and fortunes and all that makes life worth the living.

Through all this magnificent empire, this vast continental heart, like a mighty artery or system of arteries, along which pulsates the life-blood of progress and prosperity, stretches one of the grandest highways of ancient or modern times. The Chicago, Burlington & Quincy railroad is one of the giant corporations of the world. It is worthy of the region that it traverses with its four thousand miles of iron track. The world has looked on amazed at the development of this new empire of the American West. Its growth has been as wonderful as its own vastness and resources. Its grand valleys and plains which, scarcely a generation ago, were almost as much an unknown land as the shores of Zambesi or Ngami, have sprung into civilization, population, prosperity and power like the creation of an omnipotent enchanter. In the olden times such growth, such progress, such marvelous settlement and development of regions so vast and so remote would have been impossible. The old-fashioned, lumbering wagons and stage-coaches never could have transported the inhabitants and the supplies. The bare necessaries of life for such multitudes never could have been brought such vast distances over such rugged and trackless wastes, by any of the old-time methods. The enchanter's hand, the necromancer's wand, that has wrought the mighty change, is the hand, the wand, of the railroad builder and manager. The grand civilizing and developing agents have been the railroads. They have brought the vast fields and pastures, the rich mines, the boundless opportunities and resources of the great West within reach of the overcrowded human lives of the East. They have put the millions on millions of fertile western acres, that had never felt plow or harrow, within a few hours' travel of millions of hard-worked and poverty-stricken tillers of eastern flint-hills and sand-barrens. Under their magical influence the West has sprung into imperial power, as sprang Minerva from the brain of Jove, full grown and fully panoplied, without having ever known a period of childhood or pupilage.

And among all the great railways that have contributed to the grand transformation scene, that have aided in the work of turning the desert into a garden, and converting the solitary places into cities swarming with busy and prosperous people and abounding in all the refinements and luxury of the world's oldest and richest and most favored capitals and marts, none deserves a higher place, for none has done more, than the Chicago, Burlington & Quincy. And in its glorious mission of opening up and developing the newest and grandest empire on the globe, it has built up itself in a fashion without parallel.

Starting in 1849 as the "Aurora Branch," with thirteen miles of road from Aurora to Turner junction on the old Galena railway, it rose in 1854 to the control of a line from Chicago to Galesburg, a hundred and sixty-four miles. To-day, standing with one foot on the Great Lakes and the other on the Rocky Mountains, it is a veritable Colossus of Roads among the railway giants of the new world. With one mighty hand it grasps the margins of our vast inland seas, and with the other it holds the turbid floods of the Father of Waters and his grandest tributary, the swift-rolling, muddy Missouri, while with ever-extending arms of iron and links of steel it clasps to its bosom the six imperial commonwealths that form the heart of the continent. With its grand trunk lines, it binds together in manifold links of mutual interest and profitable trade, nearly all the greatest cities of the West—Chicago, St. Louis, Peoria, Burlington, Keokuk,

Rock Island, Hannibal, Quincy, St. Joseph, Kansas City, Atchison, Omaha, Council Bluffs, Lincoln and Denver. With its innumerable branches and connections it radiates from these centers to every point of the compass, opening up an empire more glorious than Roman legion or Grecian phalanx ever fought for. It constitutes a direct route of communication between such terminal points on the east as Chicago, Peoria,

CATTLE GRAZING.

View near Stanton, Iowa.

St. Louis, Denver and Leadville, and all the illimitable West and Southwest, opening to the business men of eastern cities the richest portions of Illinois, Missouri, Iowa, Nebraska, Kansas, Colorado, Montana, New Mexico and Arizona; and ere long the famed "Land of the Montezumas" will be added to the mighty list of regions made easily accessible by its untiring steeds of iron and steel. More than 200,000 square miles of the fairest and most fertile lands beneath the sun are directly tributary to it. Upon its vast network of lines, like radiant jewels on a multiplex necklace, are strung nearly 1,000 beautiful and thriving cities, towns and villages. It employs a grand army of 20,000 men. A trip over all its lines is a journey of one-sixth of the distance around the globe, a complete education in geography. Here, jump into a palatial parlor or sleeping-car at Chicago, and take a bird's-eye view of one of the grandest routes in all the world.

View near Red Oak, Iowa.

IV.

From the Great Lakes to the Rockies.

Chicago is the starting point. The seven wonders of the world have had an eighth one added to them, and its name is Chicago. Fifty years ago, a rude fort and Indian trading-post in an unknown, savage-infested wilderness. In 1840, a straggling village of 4,470 inhabitants; and in 1850, a town of but 28,260 people; to-day, it is the third city of the new world in population, the second in business importance, and the first in enterprise and promise. With a population of 600,000, and miles of the finest buildings in the world, a lake and railway commerce second only to that of New York, and with the whole grand growing West, Southwest and Northwest pouring their vast trade into its lap, Chicago's future is grand beyond the tongue or pen of uninspired prophet to portray. The next census will place it next to New York in population, and no one can say that ultimately even New York will not have to play second to the young municipal giant of the lakes.

The journeyer is standing in the magnificent Chicago, Burlington & Quincy depot, stretching from Madison street 1,100 feet in length to Adams, and from Canal street to the Chicago river, 300 feet in width. The building is one of the most imposing in the city and contains elegant waiting-rooms, dining-rooms, news depots, barber-shop and bath-rooms, and every possible convenience and comfort for travelers "All aboard!" cries the conductor, and the tourist steps on board of a train of palace sleeping, parlor and smoking cars, with a magnificent dining-car attached, and in a moment is whirling on his way out of the great city. Twelve miles through a constant succession of beautiful suburban residences, embowered in shrubbery and flowers, and Riverside is reached, on the banks of the Des Plaines river, up which Louis

Joliet and Father Marquette ascended, in 1673, from the village of the Illinois Indians to the lakes. In 1675, Father Marquette, then nearing the end of his life, passed this place, with his two faithful attendants, Pierre and Jacques, on his way to Kaskaskia, where he held a grand council with the Illinois Indians. Five hundred chiefs and old men were seated in a circle, behind them stood 1,500 youths and warriors, and in the rear of these all the women and children of the village, while Marquette preached the gospel of Jesus Christ to them. Shortly after Easter, 1675, Marquette, accompanied by a great crowd of the delighted Indians, made his last trip up the river.

Through lovely suburban towns and homes, twenty-six miles further, and Aurora comes into view. It is picturesquely situated on Fox river, which was explored by Joliet and Marquette in 1673. The first white man's cabin ever erected in the county was built on the bank of the river in 1833. Here was the starting-point of the vast Chicago, Burlington & Quincy railroad system, with the little thirteen-mile-long "Aurora Branch." The car and locomotive works at this place employ nearly 1,500 men, whose wages amount to $80,000 a month, and the annual business aggregates nearly $1,500,000.

Plano, fifteen miles further on, is the residence of Joseph Smith, the leader of the anti-polygamous Mormons, and a son of the old prophet.

Sixty-one miles from Chicago is Somonauk station, near which the Sac Indians, in 1832, massacred three families of white settlers—Halls, Daviesses and Pettigrews—numbering fifteen persons. Two young girls, Sylvia and Rachel Hall, were carried off as prisoners, but were afterward ransomed through the efforts of a Winnebago chief.

Princeton, forty-five miles onward, was long an important station on the old State road from Peoria to Galena. It was settled by colonists from Northampton, Massachusetts, and until the close of the Black Hawk war, in 1833, was much harassed by Indians.

Twenty-six miles further is passed the pretty little village of Kewanee, the name meaning in the Winnebago tongue "Prairie Hen."

Galesburg, a hundred and sixty-four miles from Chicago, is the junction of the main line of the Chicago, Burlington & Quincy road with its Peoria and Quincy divisions. It is a prosperous city of nearly 15,000 inhabitants, surrounded by a splendid farming country. It is the seat of a university, a college, and several excellent schools. It has a number of extensive manufacturing establishments, and railroad machine and repair shops.

At Burlington the majestic Mississippi is crossed on a bridge which, with its approaches, is over a mile in length, and is a masterpiece of engineering skill and taste. From the bridge a magnificent view is obtained of the river and its green dot-like islands, and of the beautiful city rising street above street in a grand semicircular amphitheatre of hills. In 1680, Father Hennepin, with two companions, Accau and Du Gay, under instructions from La Salle, explored the upper Mississippi; and about the last of March of that year, their canoe was tied up on the site of the present city of Burlington. Amid these grand hills was a favorite meeting-place and camping-ground of the warlike tribes, whose ownership of the region dates back into the misty days of legend and conjecture. Here was the last vantage ground of the famous chief, Black Hawk. Here, in the winter of 1831, he crossed the river on his way to the war against the whites, in which Abraham Lincoln, as a captain of militia, saw his first service as a soldier. And near here, after his death in October, 1838, he was buried in a sitting posture, with a staff in his hand and a tepee of stakes around and over his heroic form. Burlington is one of the most picturesque cities on the Mississippi. It has a population of about 30,000, with handsome public buildings and private residences, twelve schools and a university, a public school system that was awarded the prize at the Philadelphia Centennial Exposition. Seven railroads, two daily through lines of steamers and a number of local packets, eighty-seven manufacturing establishments whose yearly product runs near $10,000,000, mercantile houses whose annual sales amount to $20,000,000, churches of nearly all denominations found in the United States, stock-yards, elevators, breweries, foundries and mills, five newspapers, one of which is known throughout the world, one of the handsomest opera-houses in the country, and a boat-club house that is unequaled in the West. Its grain and lumber business is immense. Its people are enterprising, cultivated and hospitable, and no western or eastern city can boast more charming society. The scenery all around the city is romantic in the highest degree. The view from North Hill, in the upper part of the city, is a glorious vista of river and island, woodland, field, meadow and rolling hills. Just

Scene crossing the "Mighty Missouri," at Plattsmouth, Nebraska.

below the city is Cascade Falls, a dainty little miniature of Minnehaha. The vast rock-quarries all around the city are an almost unbroken mass of crinoids or stone lilies, the most beautiful of fossils. Many of the finest cabinets in the world have specimens from here, and almost daily parties of tourists may be seen in every direction, hammer in hand, in search of treasures rarely to be found elsewhere. A little collection made by Dr. Wachsmuth, of Burlington, was recently sold for $5,000.

The whole journey from Chicago to Burlington has been a two-hundred-and-seven-mile-long vista of beauty; a flying panorama of prosperous towns and glorious country homes; a whirling vision of the finest farming region on the globe; of handsome houses, surrounded by groves and shrubbery and flowers, waving grain-fields, orchards, vineyards, and green pastures, besprinkled with clover-blooms and dotted with sleek herds of thoroughbred cattle. The route through Iowa is much the same, except that the country is more undulating and bears more evidence of newness.

Twenty-eight miles west of Burlington is Mount Pleasant, "the Athens of Iowa," famous for its colleges and schools; and where is found in great abundance a rarely beautiful stone, the star coral, that takes the polish of marble with all the exquisite markings of coral.

A rush of forty-seven miles further west, and Ottumwa comes into view. It is one of the most important cities in Iowa, situated on the Des Moines river, whose rapids furnish water-power enough to run a thousand mills and factories. It has a population of about 12,000, having more than doubled in ten years. It is surrounded by extensive coal-fields, immense bodies of valuable timber, and as fine farming lands as ever plowshare cut furrow in. It has a hundred and ten manufacturing establishments, employing a capital of $1,032,935, and turning out in manufactured wares $3,000,000 a year. Its wholesale trade last year amounted to $2,500,000, its freight shipments were 178,440,000 pounds, and its receipts 223,116,000 pounds. Four railways, beside the Chicago, Burlington & Quincy, center in the place. It has three first-class public schools and several private ones, seventeen churches, two theatres, five newspapers, nine prominent hotels, gas-works, water-works, street railway, telephones and all the other conveniences and luxuries of metropolitanism, except a debt. It does not owe a dollar.

On through an ever-varying, beautiful succession of flourishing young towns and cities like Albia, Chariton, Creston, Villisca, Red Oak, Hastings, Glenwood, the seat of the State asylum for feeble-minded children; through a grand, far-stretching fairyland of gently rolling prairie and wildwood, rivers, lakes and brooklets; through cosy farms, with their fertile grain-fields and clustering orchards, neat houses lost in foliage and flowers, pastures in which the fat cattle and horses stand knee-deep in clover and grass; and Pacific Junction is reached. From here the main line of the Chicago, Burlington & Quincy road goes west by way of Plattsmouth, where the Missouri river is crossed on one of the grandest bridges that ever spanned the turbid flood.

Nineteen miles up the river from Pacific Junction, two hundred and ninety-four miles west of Burlington, and five hundred and one west of Chicago, the flying palaces-on-wheels sweep into the immense and stately union depot in the suburbs of Council Bluffs. Until 1846, the ground where Council Bluffs now stands was a Pottawattamie Indian reservation. About the time of their removal, the Mormons, driven out of Illinois, halted here on their strange migration westward. Brigham Young, Orson Hyde and the other leaders selected a spot on the Nebraska side of the Missouri river, about six miles north of where Omaha now stands, and calling it Winter Quarters, established a settlement of some 15,000 people. The Indians compelled them to recross to the Iowa side, and they settled on and around the site of the present city of Council Bluffs, which they called Kanesville, in honor of Thomas L. Kane, a brother of the Arctic explorer, Dr. Elisha Kent Kane, who had through the eastern press denounced the savagery of the murder by the Illinoisans of the Mormon prophet, Joe Smith. Kane went into the late war as commander of the Pennsylvania "Bucktail Regiment," and led a brigade with distinction. A battalion of three hundred of these Mormons volunteered for the Mexican war, and served heroically in the famous overland expedition under Philip St. George Cooke, Sterling Price and A. W. Doniphan. A postoffice was established at Kanesville, now Council Bluffs, in 1848. This was the great crossing-place on the Missouri of the California gold-seekers in 1849 and the two succeeding years. The Mormons set out on their pilgrimage to the New Jerusalem at Salt Lake in 1847, and most of them followed in detachments between that year and 1850. The name of Kanesville was changed to Council Bluffs in

1853, and the town proper was laid off in 1854. It now has a population of over 20,000. Seven great railways converge within its borders. During the past year 103,646 car-loads of freight

View approaching Council Bluffs, Iowa.

was received in the city, the total tonnage reaching the vast figures of 2,072,920,000 pounds. Council Bluffs handled 600,000 bushels of grain during the year, and 259,495 head of cattle, sheep and hogs. The improvements in the city last year footed up over $1,000,000. The State asylum for the deaf and dumb is located here. There are eight public schools, and a number of excellent private institutions. The city has many handsome public and private buildings, hotels, opera-houses, churches, street railway in every direction, several prosperous manufactories, and large elevators, and is growing solidly and surely.

Leaving the union depot at Council Bluffs, the train speeds across a magnificent iron bridge that spans the swift-rolling, muddy Missouri, and in a few minutes lands its living cargo in the depot at Omaha.

There are four cities in the United States that claim with reason the title of "Magic Cities." They are Chicago, Illinois; Denver and Leadville, Colorado ; and Omaha, Nebraska. On Saturday, July 21, 1804, the expedition of Lewis and Clark, sent out by the administration of President Jefferson to explore the vast unknown regions of the Northwest, landed at Plattsmouth, twenty miles below where Omaha now stands, and camped for the night. Next day, the party, consisting of forty-two men, marched ten miles and camped on the site of the present town of Bellevue, Sarpy county. Here they spent five days repairing equipments, dressing skins and arranging for a council with the Indians. A grand pow-wow was held August 2, on the spot where the government in 1819 established Fort Atkinson, afterward called Fort Calhoun. The town of Fort Calhoun now occupies the site. It lies sixteen miles above Omaha in a direct line, and forty miles by the river. Lewis and Clark called the place Council Bluffs, on account of the council held by them with the Indians, and of its convenience to the Otoes, Pawnees, Pawnee Loups, Sioux and Mahas or Omahas. The Iowa city, which has since appropriated the name, is not near the scene of the council from which it is derived.

The present site of Omaha was entered as a homestead or pre-emption claim in 1853, by William D. Brown, who had for two or three years been ferrying the California gold-hunters across the river at this point. Omaha was founded in 1854. Up to that time it had simply been known as the "Lone Tree Ferry." To-day, a handsomely built city of 40,000 inhabitants crowns the magnificent bluffs, which then were in an unknown land. Nine railways virtually center in the city, one of which, the Burlington & Missouri River road, a part of the great Chicago, Burlington & Quincy system, has been one of the grandest agencies in the marvelous development of Nebraska. Its land grant embraced a vast tract of 2,500,000 acres of the richest and most beautiful lands in the Platte and Republican valleys. It is estimated that this company alone has added 250,000 to the population of the State, and it still has 500,000 acres of the finest lands in the world for sale at from two to ten dollars an acre on long time and easy terms. The Missouri river is spanned at Omaha by a magnificent bridge that cost $1,600,000. The situation of the city is strikingly picturesque, with an amphitheatre of lofty bluffs sweeping around behind it in a grand semicircle. The city's manufactures amount to $20,000,000 a year, the Union Pacific car shops alone covering thirty acres of ground, employing nearly 2,000 hands, and turning out annually $3,000,000 worth of work. The pork-packing and meat-canning business amounts to over $2,500,000 a year, and the product of the breweries and distilleries to nearly $7,000,000. The Omaha smelting-works are, with two exceptions, the largest in the world, their business last year amounting to over $6,000,000. The live stock trade aggregates nearly $9,000,000 a year, and its wholesale and commission trade to upwards of $15,000,000. Her schools are one of Omaha's special prides. The high-school building, which cost $250,000, standing on the summit of a lofty hill in the rear of the city, on the site where stood the old State Capitol building, its tall spire reaching three hundred and ninety feet above the level of the river, is the most conspicuous object in the city, and can be seen for miles in every direction. Besides this splendid institution, there are five handsome public schools, an Episcopal seminary for young ladies, a Catholic college and the Nebraska business college. There are five public libraries, twenty-eight churches, elegant opera-houses and hotels, a government building that cost $350,000, fourteen English papers, five of them daily; one Danish, one Bohemian and five German papers. The improvements during last year aggregated $2,241,000, and the rush of building still goes on. No city in the Union is growing faster in proportion to its present population, and every indication promises a grand future for Omaha. At Council Bluffs, Montana, California, and Oregon passengers by the Chicago, Burlington & Quincy are transferred to the Union Pacific in the union depot.

Leaving the immense union depot, swarming day and night with emigrants, home-seekers from every land and nation, the journeyer westward by the great Burlington Route finds himself whirling along the margin of the Big Muddy over the splendidly equipped and ballasted track of the Burlington & Missouri River road. Sixteen miles of flying river and meadow and far-stretching grain-field on one side, and romantic bluffs and hills on the other, puts the train at Oreapolis. Here the Omaha line joins the main Chicago, Burlington & Quincy line, which crosses the Missouri river at Plattsmouth, the landing-point of Lewis and Clark's romantic exploring expedition seventy-eight years ago. The bridge and its approaches over the Missouri at Plattsmouth is nearly two miles long, and is one of the most notable pieces of engineering in the country.

Passenger Station at Lincoln, Nebraska, and view of the Great Salt Basin.

At Oreapolis the beautiful Platte river is crossed, and the train flies on through an enchanting succession of waving fields of grain, groves of elms and cottonwoods, and vast natural pastures reaching to the horizon on every side. Tasteful farm-houses and young orchards dot all the landscape with sweet suggestions of home in what scarce twenty years ago was a wilderness almost unbroken. A two hours' run from Oreapolis brings into view the spires and towers of Lincoln, the capital of the State, a beautifully built and prosperous city of

15,000 inhabitants. It is in the center of the rich and fertile South Platte country, as it is called ; here too are also found the salt basins, where salt-making is carried on. There are many handsome buildings in the place, among them the State Capitol, the State university and agricultural college and the Nebraska hospital for the insane, the United States postoffice and court-house, which cost $150,000, and the high-school building, which cost $40,000. Besides these there are numerous elegant business blocks and private residences. Three divisions of the Burlington & Missouri River road center here, and in the magnificent depot are the offices of the land department of the company, a department which has done more perhaps than any other agency in bringing in settlers and developing the grand resources of the State. The State penitentiary is located just south of the city. There are a number of flourishing manufacturing establishments. The city is charmingly situated on high, rolling hills, and is growing with wonderful rapidity. Divisions of the Burlington & Missouri River road lead from here to Columbus and Central City on the Union Pacific road and the Platte river, and to Nebraska City, Nemaha and Atchison on the Missouri. Ninety-seven miles further, along the divide between the Platte and Republican rivers, through a land of wheat and corn fields, orchards and rich pastures, everywhere watered by pure streams, and beautified by groves of willows, elms, maples and cottonwoods, and dotted with thriving young towns like Crete, Exeter, Fairmont, Grafton and Harvard, brings the pilgrim to Hastings, where one arm of the Burlington & Missouri road reaches out to Kearney on the Union Pacific and Platte river, and the other to Red Cloud on the Republican.

Red Cloud takes its name from the famous Sioux Chief who was born here. It is a flourishing little town of about 1,200 people, on the Burlington air-line from Chicago to Denver. From Red Cloud west, the route for over two hundred miles follows the windings of the great Republican valley, than which the world contains no more fertile and beautiful body of agricultural and pastoral lands. All the most nutritious grasses grow wild in rank luxuriance, and there are many acres yet untaken and open to all the world. In these vast unclaimed pastures tens of thousands of cattle and sheep find rich abundance all the year round, without expense to their owners. It costs little to start in a business which, with any ordinary care, yields a fortune in five or six years.

The Republican valley was historic ground generations before the first white settler ever planted his feet upon the eastern shores of the United States. In 1541, seventy-nine years before the landing of the pilgrims on Plymouth rock, Coronado, the lieutenant of Cortez, set out from Mexico with eight hundred cavalry, to subdue the seven cities of Cibola, that rumor said lay far to the north and were very rich. Some mythical personage appeared to him somewhere near Santa Fé with stories of fabulous wealth of a land far northeast. Inflamed with avarice and ambition he pushed his way into the Republican valley, leaving perpetual remembrances of his march in the names of rivers and places along the route, Las Animas, Las Cruces, Espiritu Santo, San Jose, San Joaquin and many others. Near Riverton, on the Burlington & Missouri River road, west of Red Cloud, remains of ancient Spanish saddles, stirrups and portions of armor have been found. Here Coronado heard of a great river to the north, and discovered the Platte. He was still told of a greater river to the eastward. He started to find it, but was driven back by the Indians, and without having seen it he named it the " River of the Holy Ghost." It was, of course, the Missouri. Coronado returned to Mexico, reorganized his forces and set out again to occupy and hold this magnificent garden-like region, but was defeated and killed by the natives before he accomplished his great design.

Thirteen miles west of Red Cloud is Riverton, in the center of the " Nebraska Geyser System," a continuation of the great Yellowstone Park geyser bed. These in Nebraska have long been extinct, but the strange looking cones and chimneys, craters and scape-pipes still remain as perfect as in the far-back period when they spouted and sputtered as though Beelzebub was making soup of sinners at their deep-down furnace fires.

Near Republican City, twenty-eight miles further west, amid a wild tangle of geysers and curious cliffs, are found the remains of countless mastodons, mammoths and other extinct races of animals, among them a woolly elephant with long, curling tusks like those of a gigantic boar, the bones showing that the monster must have been nearly twenty feet in height. The whole region abounds with these strange relics of monsters that browsed, when the world was young, amid sky-sweeping groves of sequoias, of which the big trees of California are degenerate descendants.

View on the Platte River.

At Arapahoe, thirty-nine miles on toward sunset, is one of the most remarkable deposits of silicates in the world, left by the geysers of long ago.

Culbertson, fifty-one miles onward, is in the center of an almost boundless cattle range, where stock by hundreds of thousands of head can be raised at comparatively little expense, grass all the year, abundant water, mild climate, and even salt springs for salting, leaving nothing to be desired. Thousands of square miles are open to any and every comer with his herd of cattle or drove of sheep.

Eight miles west of Culbertson is Massacre Cañon, where, about ten years ago, the Sioux surprised and slaughtered a large number of Pawnees. Skulls and bones of the victims are still to be seen strewn in the wild gulch.

Shortly after crossing the Colorado line near Collinsville is the scene of the bloody battle of Arickaree Fork, between the Indians and United States troops.

On, on, through a region which the Chicago, Burlington & Quincy road has just opened up to civilization and improvement. Through far-reaching vistas of pasture-lands, and here and there a dreary stretch of alkali and sage-brush. Through a region, of great possibilities, where everything as yet is new and crude. On, on, across innumerable little tributaries of the Republican and the Platte, "arroyos" as they call them here, foaming torrents in the rainy season, dry beds of sand at other times, but always yielding water to any one who will dig a few feet for it.

On, till at last the grand Rocky Mountains loom into view, and with a shrill shriek of delight the locomotive rushes into the Queen City of the Rockies. Denver, a municipal miracle; an infant in years, a giant in development. Unheard of, unknown even as a wild, frontier camping-place for scouts and prospectors, until the Pike's Peak gold craze of 1858-9. To-day, one of the most prosperous, beautiful and famous cities of the new world. Standing on a beautiful high plateau, 5,244 feet above the level of the sea, and sixteen miles from the foothills which, in the pure, transparent Colorado atmosphere, seem hardly a half-hour's walk away, the site of the city could not be more charming. It commands a view of the cloud-capped Rocky Mountains for three hundred miles. Seventy miles north-west, in plain sight is Long's Peak, 14,271 feet, or two and three-quarter miles, high. Far away to the southward is Pike's Peak, 14,147 feet high, and all the space between is cleft by mighty peaks, many of them glistening beneath their crowns of everlasting ice and snow. As a gifted writer, gazing on these majestic scenes, exclaims: Imagine the whole of New England lifted bodily a mile above the sea-level; add 3,500 feet to the height of Mount Washington; put in a dozen other peaks of equal elevation; throw in, promiscuously, a couple of hundred other peaks from ten to fourteen thousand feet high; exaggerate the Notch, the Pool and Flume a dozen times, and multiply them by a score; add parks larger than any of her States; and gardens filled with quaint statuary fashioned by the attrition of time and wind and wave; run tunnels here and there into the mountains, and sink numberless shafts a thousand feet below the surface; underlay the whole vast area with miles on miles of gold and silver; shut off the misty breezes of the sea, and substitute the pure, exhilarating atmosphere of the plains; smite rock-ribbed mountain-sides, and call forth numberless mineral springs of great curative virtues; and then you have a faint approximation only of the boundless attractions which Colorado offers to its visitors.

In the midst, the very heart of these sublime scenes, Denver sits enthroned, beauteous queen of a surpassingly lovely realm. Sprung from the nothingness of twenty years ago, from the villagehood of ten years ago, she claims to-day a population of 65,000, and has 50,000, an increase of 15,000 since the census of 1880. Over 1,000 buildings, aggregating nearly $3,000,000 in cost, were erected last year. The public and private buildings are on a scale of magnificence unsurpassed in the country, outside of New York or Chicago. Tabor opera-house, built by a man who in 1877 kept a little country store in Leadville, cost $875,000, and has no superior in the Union. Tabor block cost nearly $300,000, the Windsor hotel $300,000, and a government building to cost $500,000 is to be put up at once. The St. James, American and Inter-ocean, Charpiot's and the Brunswick are all hotels that would be creditable in any city. Denver is a port of delivery, and has a branch of the United States mint. There are many elegant churches, St. John's Episcopal cathedral having cost $125,000, the First Presbyterian and Central Baptist edifices being specially noticeable. The Catholics are preparing to build a magnificent cathedral. The Argo smelting works, owned by Senator N. P. Hill and Boston parties, is the largest establishment of the kind in America. Denver has three morning daily newspapers, "The Tribune," "The News" and "The Republican;" two evening

dailies, "The Times" and "The World;" one German daily
and ten or twelve weeklies.   One of the weekly papers is "The
Great West," edited by the famous Brick Pomeroy, who has just
built a $30,000 residence here, and whose career would make a

Scene on the Republican River.

dozen yellow-back romances.   The city has miles of street railway, fire-alarm telegraph, telephones and electric light, is supplied
with pure water by the Holly system of water-works, and a considerable part of it heated by a steam heating company.   A circle

railroad runs entirely round the place, about fifteen miles. The streets are very fine, eighty feet wide, of natural gravel and ornamented by 200,000 shade trees, which are daily watered. Broadway, the fashionable drive, is a mile and a half long and a hundred feet wide, and every afternoon swarms with fast teams and handsome equipages. The fair grounds, with a splendid half-mile race-track, are near the city. There are no parks, and surrounded as Denver is with so many of the grandest scenes on earth, there is little need of any. Denver is the centering-place of some of the most important railroads upon the continent: the Chicago, Burlington & Quincy—"Burlington Route," as it is popularly called, the only direct through line to Chicago; three divisions of the Union Pacific, including the Kansas Pacific; the Denver & Rio Grande, opening up some of the most gorgeous mountain scenery that human eyes ever beheld; the Denver & South Park; the Denver & New Orleans, and the Denver, Utah & Pacific. It is the central point from which all Colorado business and travel radiate. Near at hand and easy of access are all the famous scenes of the Garden of the Gods, Boulder and Clear Creek Cañons, North, Middle and Estes Parks; all the great bonanza mines of Leadville, Georgetown, Golden and Central; and the miracle-working medicinal waters of Colorado, Idaho and Manitou Springs, iron, sulphur, soda, magnesia, every variety of chalybeates, hot, cold and tepid, duplicating all the far-famed waters of Bath and Ems and Baden-Baden abroad, and those of Saratoga, Blue Lick and the various sulphur springs at home. The air is dry, pure and invigorating. No dew falls, no dampness or miasma is ever known. Asthma finds immediate and permanent relief, catarrh and hay-fever disappear at once and forever, even the oldest chronic cases being promptly benefited. Consumption in all its earlier stages may be cured by this balmy, healing air, and all the grand and glorious surroundings charm the spirit, while the body is being restored to health. There is no reason why this region should not become the world's greatest sanitarium and most fashionable resort. It has every advantage and the beauty of all the other noted health and pleasure resorts combined, and all on a far grander scale.

Denver has completed this year (1882), at a cost of $100,000, a grand international mining exposition building, in which was held, August 1st to September 30th, one of the most extensive and interesting exhibitions of the kind that ever took place in the annals of mines and mining.   Every part of the United States, Mexico, the Central American States, South America's principal mining provinces and Australia were represented

Massacre Cañon, Nebraska.

V.

The Heart of the Continent.

Such is a trip over the great Chicago, Burlington & Quincy railroad, from the Lakes to the Rockies, the vast resources that lie along its mighty line, and the wonders that surround its terminal points. It would take volumes to enumerate and describe in detail all its features and attractions, even to call the roll of the cities it brings close together in time, if not in distance.

Returning eastward from Denver it has a line running the whole length of the fertile Republican valley, by way of Red Cloud, Atchison and Kansas City, to St. Louis. This last city, the metropolis of Missouri and of the Mississippi valley, is the terminus of two grand divisions of the Chicago, Burlington & Quincy road. St. Louis was first settled in 1763, by adventurous French traders. Twenty-five miles below the junction of the great Mississippi and Missouri rivers, and one hundred and eighty-seven miles above the junction of the Ohio and Mississippi, this great city has a royal position for commercial importance. It virtually commands over 10,000 miles of navigation on the mightiest rivers of the globe. The vast system of railways, which centers here, reaches out its iron arms to every region of the continent. The trade of Missouri, Texas, Arkansas and Indian territory, and of a large portion of Louisiana, Mississippi, western Tennessee and Kentucky, Kansas and New Mexico should naturally come to St. Louis. The city has a population of about 400,000, handsome public and private buildings, beautiful parks and gardens, some of which are deservedly famed throughout the country, stately and elegant churches, many of the finest schools, of all grades, in the United States, a university that is perhaps not excelled by any in America, extensive libraries, academies of art and design, newspapers that are scarcely surpassed in the world, and all the institutions and characteristics of a great natural metropolis, the fifth city of the republic. It is famed for its solid wealth, the substantial character of its business men, and the culture, refinement and hospitality of its society. Its commerce is daily increasing in volume and extent, magnificent buildings are going up in every part of its bounds, a rush of improvement is visible everywhere, and every indication presages a glorious future, commercial, financial, political and social, for the imperial city of the grandest valley on the globe.

Another of the eastern termini of the Chicago, Burlington & Quincy railroad is Peoria, a city itself worthy of many pages of description. Situated on the site of La Salle's ancient fort of "Crèvecœur," or Broken Heart, there is no broken heartedness about it or its citizens. It is one of the wealthiest and most prosperous cities of 40,000 people on the continent. It has eleven lines of railroad, its manufacturing and mercantile business last year aggregated $481,048,572, an increase of $86,286,552 over the preceding year. Its distilleries alone paid, during the year, $12,453,872 of internal revenue, more than is paid by any other revenue district in the United States. The city last year handled over 28,000,000 bushels of grain, its weekly clearings averaged over $1,000,000, it is beautifully built, growing rapidly and prospering beyond all description.

Another city on the Chicago, Burlington & Quincy trans-continental-heart line is Des Moines, the beautiful capital of Iowa, risen from a hundred and twenty-seven inhabitants in 1846, to 27,000 in 1882. Seven railways center in the city and two others are being built. The surrounding country is of unsurpassed fertility, and coal and timber abound. The manufactures of the city last year amounted to $12,738,781, its wholesale trade to $20,681,781, its grain and produce trade to $2,770,250, its coal trade to $1,175,750, and the improvements made during the year reached a grand total of $3,529,979. With a wide-awake, intelligent, enterprising population, and with an infinitude of natural advantages and resources, Des Moines is destined to play no unimportant part in the grand drama of northwestern progress.

Call the roll of great western cities, Chicago, St. Louis, Kansas City, Peoria, Burlington, Quincy, St. Joseph, Rock Island, Keokuk, Davenport, Des Moines, Atchison, Council Bluffs, Omaha, Lincoln and Denver. All here, and all on the lines of the Briareus-handed, hundred-armed Chicago, Burlington & Quincy railroad.

Ask for all the richest regions in the six grandest States of the American Great West; and they all respond: Here, along the lines of the Chicago, Burlington & Quincy. Inquire for the

Platte Cañon, Colorado.

most glorious health and pleasure resorts upon the globe; and the answer is: In Colorado at the western end of the Chicago, Burlington & Quincy. To the traveler on business or for pleasure, going from the east to the west, it is the only through line. To the journeyer from the great lakesides to the Rocky Mountains, it is the only line, direct, owning its road clear through, and running its own cars. From Chicago to Denver, it is the first and only through line, and by many miles shorter than any of the broken and disjointed competing routes. To the grand scenery and health-giving air and medicated waters of the Rocky Mountain Wonderland, it is the only direct route under one management. To the eastern seeker for a home and a bonanza fortune, it affords the shortest, quickest, cheapest and best route to the broad valleys and prairies, the free pastures and grain-fields, and the daily developing mines of the marvelous Far West. To the eastern and southern summer tourist and refugee from torrid heats and lowland miasmas, it presents the most direct and luxuriously appointed highway to all the glorious loitering-places of the American Alps, where snow-capped peaks are ever in sight, where every breath is full of vigor; where the eye and heart may feast on all that is most sublime and magnificent in mountain, valley, lake, river, cataract, crag and cañon; and where Nature, from her strange, hidden laboratories, pours forth her wondrous healing floods that need no angel's pinion to stir them, as did Bethesda's pool of old, to give them potency for the relief of human woes. To the Colorado cattle shipper, it offers by far the most direct and convenient line to the great markets of the world. To everybody and anybody, bound from anywhere to anywhere else, to trans-continental tourists, as well as to local shippers and journeyers, the Chicago, Burlington & Quincy railroad offers every inducement and accommodation. It is the business man's route between the east and west. It is the artist's and tourist's route to all that is most gorgeous in scenery on the continent. It is the homeseeker's route to millions on millions of acres of free farming and grazing lands. It is the stock-raiser's route to cattle ranges and sheep pastures that cost nothing and are only fenced by the horizon. It is the fortune-hunter's route to all the bonanza mines, present and to come. It is the invalid's route to the world's most glorious sanitarium.

The Chicago, Burlington & Quincy Company, one of the wealthiest and most powerful corporations in the world, with a capital stock that runs far up into the tens of millions, and managed by able, progressive, liberal men who stand in the front rank of their profession, can and does offer every possible inducement and convenience to the journeying public, no matter where that public journeys from or journeys to. Owning and controlling over 4,000 miles of splendid track, much of it double and nearly all of it laid with the finest steel rails, its managers have equipped it with lavish disregard of costs, but the greatest care for the comfort and convenience of their patrons. Magnificent iron bridges span all the rivers on its route, and palatial parlor, stateroom, sleeping and dining cars fly along its smooth, stone-ballasted track at a high rate of speed without a jolt or a discomfort—sumptuous hotels on wheels, where one can eat, drink, read or sleep at pleasure, while he skims like a bird through glorious panoramas of city and country, orchards and wildwoods, mountain, prairie, lake, valley and majestic river.

The cars run on all the lines of this model company are really marvels of ingenuity, beauty and elegance, including all the improvements of the age. Its stateroom and sleeping cars are massive in build, elegantly decorated with carving and inlaying of various colored woods, gilding and painting, and costly mirrors and curtains, and furnished with luxurious cushions, marble wash-basins and snowy towels. The beds are as clean and comfortable as those of the finest city hotels, and the weary traveler easily and delightfully dreams over two hundred and fifty miles of space. The dining-room cars, which this road was one of the first in the world to introduce, are each furnished with tables enough to accommodate thirty guests at a time. The tablecloths and napkins are of damask, fine as silk and white as snow, the silver and glassware is heavy and fine, the waiters well-trained and attentive, and the bill-of-fare as sumptuous as any journeying epicure could ask. It embraces soups, fish, game, meats, vegetables, fragrant coffee and tea, rich cream and milk, fruits, found at first-class hotels. All this catalogue of dainties to be enjoyed for seventy-five cents. No scalding of your mouth in the rush and hurry of a twenty-minute halt at a wayside tavern. All calm, leisurely enjoyment of an elegant meal in the highest style of culinary art, with thirty or forty miles of panoramic landscape

thrown in through the car window, as an æsthetic relish and
appetizer. Softly cushioned reclining-chair cars are furnished,

The Gate to the Garden of the Gods, Colorado.

without extra charge, on many of the divisions. They are provided with wash-room, towels and all other toilet conveniences,
and each one is in charge of a trusty porter, just as the sleeping-
cars are.

Let the traveler or the shipper come whence he may or go

whither he may, in all the great Heart of the Continent, from east to west or west to east, the Chicago, Burlington & Quincy railroad offers him every advantage and facility. It furnishes him a road which passes through scores of the most important cities, and thousands of miles of the richest lands and most enchanting scenes, in the West, and on which the possibility of fatal accidents is reduced to the minimum. It furnishes the fastest rate of speed to be attained on any western line, attentive employés, and swift and sure connections for every important point or region on the continent, and its fares and tariffs are always as low as the lowest.

For the shipment of freight to or from the West, it offers choice of two through lines, magnificently equipped with freight and stock cars that have every modern improvement and convenience, including refrigerators for fruit, meats and other perishable articles, and comfortable stall cars for fine grades of live-stock. Its engines are as fine as any made or used in the world, and it has all the necessary facilities to make the "Burlington Route" forever the favorite medium of trade and travel between the Great Lakes and the Rocky Mountains, the grand main artery through "The Heart of the Continent."

In the preceding pages we have endeavored to describe in a general way the inducements offered in the six great States, and the appended map will show how to reach the most important towns and cities therein. Many other questions may arise which we have been unable to cover, but we shall be only too happy to give any additional information that may be desired as to routes, rates, time of trains, lands for sale, guide books for tourists, &c., upon application either in person or by letter to the Passenger Department, Chicago, Burlington & Quincy R. R., Chicago, Ill.

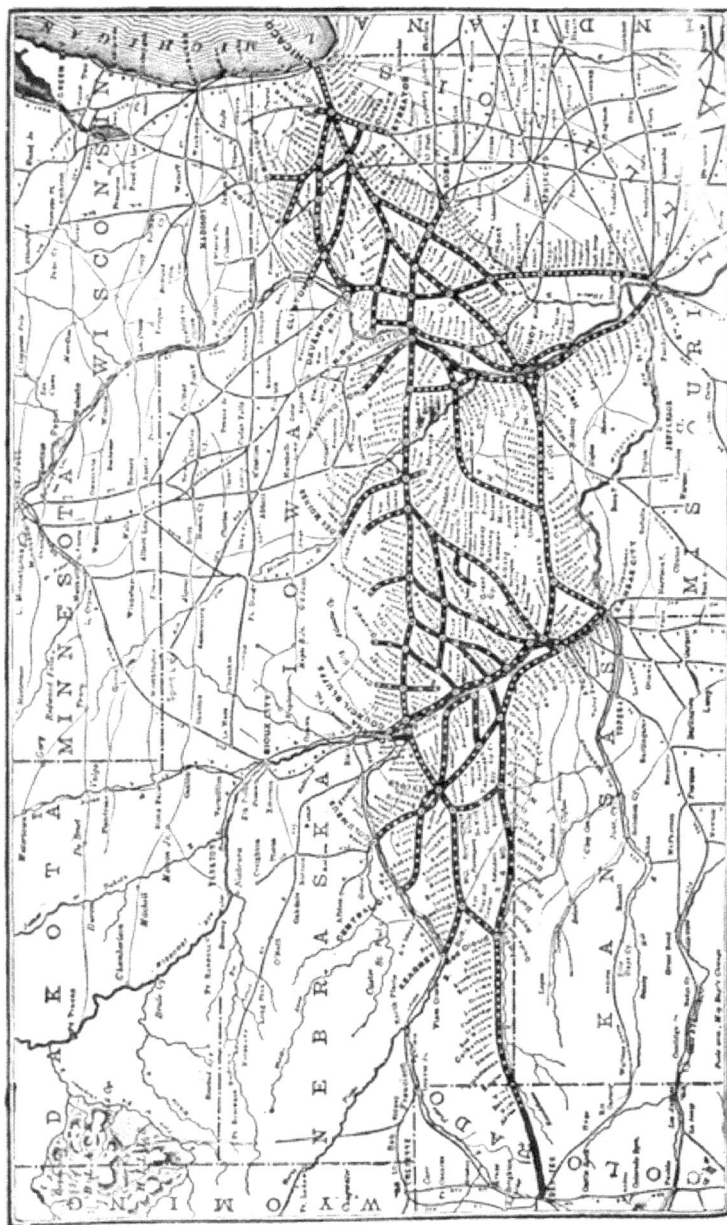

This Line offers Superior Facilities

Map of the GREAT BURLINGTON ROUTE.

Finest Equipped Railroad in the World.

And Inducements to all Classes of Travellers.

www.ingramcontent.com/pod-product-compliance
Lightning Source LLC
Chambersburg PA
CBHW021514090426

42739CB00007B/605